Dear Dad....

I don't think you understand, nor do we do a great enough job expressing (in most instances) how important you are!

We may not have worked out romantically!

We may not even like each other as humans!

We may still be together and trying to figure this thing out!

As co-parents, if we are both pulling our weight, no one parent is more important than the other.

You matter! YES, YOU DO!

The next few pages are dedicated to us working together to appreciate you and repair what's broken in us.

With Love,

A single mother

A letter to the unmarried father, from a single mother

WHAT IS A SINGLE MOTHER?
LET'S CONQUER THIS ELEPHANT FIRST

Culturally, this means a few different things. We won't dig into this, it's a divisive rabbit hole. The only thing that matters is what's recognized on legal documentation. When filling out any submission of information seeking to identify and separate you into a demographic, what do they ask?

Are you: Single? Married? Divorced? In a Domestic Partnership? Other?

I have never seen legal binding documents that ask, specifically, are you a "single parent"? I have however, reviewed documents referring to joint and sole custody.

Single is a marital status.

To be a single parent means that you are an unmarried parent.

Definition of *single parent*

: a parent who lives with a child or children and no husband, wife, or partner

(source: Merriam-Webster dictionary, 2020)

Let's move on!

What are some of the messages that you wish society would stop sending about single mothers?

_____
_____
_____
_____
_____
_____
_____
_____
_____
_____
_____
_____

WHAT IS COPARENTING?
WE HAVE TO LEVEL SET TO MOVE ON

Definition of co-*parent(ing)*

: a divorced or separated parent who shares equally with the other parent in the custody and care of a child.

(source: dictionary.com, 2020)

I'll leave this here. Stay with me, I'm going somewhere.

Let's move on!

What are some of the messages that you wish society would stop sending about co-parenting?

_____
_____
_____
_____
_____
_____
_____
_____
_____
_____
_____
_____
_____
_____
_____
_____
_____
_____
_____
_____
_____
_____
_____
_____

WE NEED YOU!
NO MATTER HOW WE ACT

Dad, we need you! One more time for the men in the back who have heard they're worthless, we can do this alone or they can't get it right! I don't care what she says in anger, hurt or frustration, I'm telling you, we need you! Most women were never taught about how emotionally fragile men are. In the same cases, healthy examples of what a man should be was absent from the home. Depending on which generation you were raised by, here's what your definition of a man looked like: *the emotionally absent provider, the physically absent provider, the emotionally & physically absent provider or he was just absent.*

The emotionally absent provider brought home the bacon and never publicly shared a loving sentiment. The perception was that his provision was his expression of love.

The physically absent provider sent the bacon home, and never came with it. If he didn't work long hours, the family didn't eat. The perception was that he didn't prioritize time with family.

The emotionally & physically absent provider was perceived as neither prioritizing time with family or expressing love outside of paying bills and buying gifts.

In relationships we spend our time together convincing each other that we aren't what our partner is used to. We're competing with years of experience unless they did the healing work to address that baggage. In most cases, we don't know what we don't know about certain preconceived notions and expectations until we experience something completely contrary, to what we know.

Which provider type do you most identify with? Why? Where is there opportunity for you to grow?

_____
_____
_____
_____
_____

WHAT DO YOU THINK WE WANT?
NO SERIOUSLY, I WANT TO KNOW

You! Dad! It's truly that simple! We want the man we chose. The man we saw in all his perfection an imperfection. The man that chased us to get us. That same effort can't die, within reason. Is it mutual? Do we need to maintain the same consistency as much as reasonably possible? Absolutely! However, we're talking about you today! Single Moms have a 31-day affirmation, written by me, that's dealing with all their mess and some things about you, too!! So back to you. Yes, men are expected to be the provider. That looks different in different homes. Some traditional. Some not so much. What works in your home is solely up to the family who must live with it. No one else. Communication can get you where you need to be with that. And that word, communication, is the quickest route to a happy, healthy, functioning family.

We WANT you. We NEED you, to talk.

The woman in your life is supposed to be your partner in crime. When we're meeting each other's expressed needs, this is easy. It's when we shut down and leverage alternative outlets that we start having problems. Often, when we lose the ability to talk, we lose the ability to move forward.

How open are you with your significant other? Why/not? Where can you present an opportunity to be more transparent?

_____
_____
_____
_____
_____
_____
_____
_____
_____
_____
_____
_____

**YOUR ARE NOT YOUR FATHER?
OR ARE YOU? IT'S YOUR CHOICE**

What's your relationship like with your dad?

Do you want to be like him?

Do you want the relationship that you had with him, with your child(ren)? Why/not?

What can you do to make sure that that you have/don't have that relationship?

This is extremely personal.

Let's just reflect here and we'll reconnect in the next section.

_____
_____
_____
_____
_____
_____
_____
_____
_____
_____
_____
_____
_____
_____
_____
_____
_____
_____
_____
_____
_____
_____
_____
_____

YOU ARE NOT A FAILURE!
YOU MADE A MISTAKE

Failure is an activity, not a destination! I am certain someone else said that first, don't tell them that I am using it *wink, wink*. Although I am not sure who coined the phrase, I do know that they were right.

They are right. Parenting is hard. Relationships are hard.

You won't get everything right either. You're not perfect. You're not expected to be. You're human. Anyone who doesn't comprehend this basic tenet, isn't worth your time, no matter who they are.

You can only do your best. When you feel like you aren't, it's on you to press yourself to the next level. The love in your life, your kids, family, etc can encourage however you are the only one who can make you move.

It's all personal. Be kind to yourself. Be gentle with yourself. You don't know what you don't know, and you'll figure it out.

Parenting and love are on the job training!

Take it one day at a time.

In what areas are you extremely hard on yourself? Why? How can you still reach the goal without breaking yourself down?

_____
_____
_____
_____
_____
_____
_____
_____
_____
_____
_____
_____

**SHE WAS NOT THE ONE!
AND NOW THERE'S A CHILD**

Men get hurt. The woman isn't always the prize, honestly there are just as many bad women as there are deemed men. There are feelings associated with bad relationships. There's a residue left when it's over.

Anything that a woman can experience, there's a similar experience for a man.

The breakup stings. The loss of a child stings. The inability to support the way you would like to, stings. Being consulted after the fact, stings. I can go on. I think you get the point though. Unfortunately, how to move forward as a co-parent with someone who has played a part in breaking your heart is why we're here. The wounds behind these types of feelings are where the "single mother" stigma was born.

Sharing responsibilities with someone you still like can be easy.

Co-existing with someone who you have visions of dragging behind a car is a different story. Fix your face. I have heard stories. I have also seen the news. I have witnessed the extremes to which visions can go.

Nothing matters more than that child. Not her open wounds or bitterness. Not your broken heart or rage. None of it matters more than the kids. I am a parent, 2/3 or my children were born out of an unhealthy relationship, 1/3 out of a healed one. I have seen the differences that simply checking myself has made in both scenarios. The younger years for my oldest two were tough and I looked for every opportunity to not deal with their father. However, he was still their father and although he wasn't what I needed or what was best for me, he had a role to play in their lives. A role outside of me. As parents, the best thing that we can do is let that play out on its own. When you are the **Rockstar dad** that we know you are, you must trust the process. Stay out of the mess! It's hard. It's extremely hard. It's also extremely necessary. Children are not stupid. Let me say it again, your children are not stupid. Remain consistent.

Where is there an opportunity for you to heal? What needs to happen for you to start healing? What can you do differently to support/maintain your healing?

DEAR DAD...

I'd like to first say that I love you. No matter what road we traveled to get where we are, I love you as the father of my child. I appreciate what you have tried to do for our child and see your consistent effort. If you keep making strides to be the best dad that you can be, I will always support you. It won't necessarily look the way you want it to. However, the support is there. Once our relationship changed, certain dynamics had to change. As we continue to grow in our separate directions, those dynamics will consistently shift. One thing that I promise is that we'll remain on the same page for our child(ren).

Our styles are different. Our roles are different. I expect there'll be disagreement around tactics and appropriate times. It's life. We're feeling through this thing together. Neither of us may have had the greatest parenting examples growing up. If we didn't pick up what to do over the years, we can say we learned what not to. Let's start there. We must talk to each other. We can't parent in silos. We'll confuse our children. They'll leverage our discord and work to play us against each other. Children are little opportunists, especially once they become teens.

Whether we live under one roof or in separate states, we must present a unified front.

We dropped the ball on us. Let's forgive each other and apply those lessons to future relationships. Let's not work to repeatedly live in dysfunction. Let's work together to build healthy people. Afterall, we are our child's first example of everything. How we carry ourselves dictates how they carry themselves in the world. That's a lot of responsibility. What a weight to bear! We can't do this alone.

Let's work together. The future of our community depends on it!

With love,

A Single (unmarried) Mom

THANK YOU FOR READING!

1. Please leave a review on amazon!
2. Pick up A Mother's Love; 31 days of Affirmations for Single Mothers for a mom you know OR Parenting is a love-hate relationship for yourself!
3. Follow the SMNPCE INC (Single Mother's Navigating Parenting | Careers | Entrepreneurship INC, a 501c3) Facebook page!

www.ingramcontent.com/pod-product-compliance
Lightning Source LLC
Chambersburg PA
CBHW022000290426
44108CB00012B/1157